A Bird'

A Bird's Idea of Flight

DAVID HARSENT

FABER & FABER

First published in 1998
by Faber & Faber Ltd
Bloomsbury House
74–77 Great Russell Street
London WC1B 3DA
This paperback edition first published in 2017

Photoset by Wilmaset Ltd, Wirral
Printed in England by Martins the Printers, Berwick-upon-Tweed

A CIP record for this book
is available from the British Library

ISBN 978–0–571–33007–2

2 4 6 8 10 9 7 5 3 1

To Alice & Fred

⌣

Thanne lyd mine hus uppen mine nos.
Anon. (13th century)

⌣

. . . folly. Thoughtlessness. Extravagance. Immaturity.
Foolishness. Irrationality. Insecurity. Frivolity. Spontaneity.
Pleasure. Levity. Lack of discipline. Inconsideration.
Exhibitionism. Rashness. Frenzy. Unrestrained excess.
Ridiculous expenditure or act. Carelessness in promises.
Inattentiveness to important details. Beginning an adventure.
Infatuation. Indiscretion. Craze. Passion. Obsession. Mania.
Tendency to start a project without carefully considering all
the details. Initiative. Enthusiasm. Reluctance to listen to
advice from other people.
Stuart R. Kaplan, *The Classical Tarot*

⌣

Your eyes fall in, your teeth fall out,
Your brains'll trickle down your snout.
Anon. (20th century)

Acknowledgements

Some of these poems have appeared, sometimes in different versions and with different titles, in *Descant* (Canada), *The Printer's Devil*, *Epoch* (USA), the *London Review of Books*, *New Writing 5* (edited by Christopher Hope and Peter Porter), the programme for Poetry International 1996 (South Bank Centre), *The Rialto*, *Stand*, *Thumbscrew*, and the *Times Literary Supplement*.

Poem III refers to Rembrandt's *The Anatomy Lesson of Doctor Deyman*; Poem VII uses images from some photographs by Peter Hujar; Poem XVII trades off Dunbar's *Lament for the Makaris*; Poem XXIII refers to Joseph Wright's *An Experiment with a Bird in the Air Pump*.

Contents

1 The Archivist

I found him, as they said I would, walled-up
by tree-calf and buckram.
Anglepoise, lectern, stool,
stylus, dividers ... He crouched
in a funnel of ivory light;
I heard the creak of vellum,
then my own breathing, then his — a rich
cackle of tar rising
in either lung. He sifted the arcana,
part-chanted, part-sung —
dates and times as usual, the usual rhymes
but also the way a name
might sometimes become divisible by number.

'Your children admire you. Worse than that,
your wives kept back
all the old stuff you thought you'd thrown away.
Your parents loved you in their secret selves.
Because you hated them they lean
towards you to apologise.' He clicked
his tongue: 'There's little more to learn, but why
did you come to me? You could have got
this much and more from any girl
with a pack of cards, a gift-
shop crystal and a borrowed shawl.'

~

As he bent back to trawl
the page, I heard a rustle like something
stirring a fall of leaves, and a worm
came out of his head, a thin
filament, breaking the skin
of the waxy crescent
just behind his ear, nosing the air
for the hint of burning
back along the stack.
'You have wasted your life.
I can't give news of the journey
you want to undertake,
but everything here says *pointless*,
ill-advised; look for yourself ... ' He was cupping
a mirror; I saw my image flow
from the glass to the sieve of his fingers.
He spread his hands: 'What else ... ?
What else do you want to know?'

11 Archaeology

Two men, one in army-surplus
jungle greens,

the other wearing
his slicker like a cloak,

are seen on a sloping track.
We follow them until

they astonish us
by sidling into the shoulder of the hill.

~

One calls, 'I'm face to face
with the Devil's younger brother –'

so when the horns
and beard and whiplash tongue

of a gargoyle crash
into focus across the void,

and the wind draws off a note
from the mossy bell,

it's clear they've found the site
of the buried cathedral.

~

Our best view of the men is when they abseil
down two hundred feet

from cupola to nave, and light
strikes through the borehole,

finding the famous, vast stained-glass
window; at once they're lapped

in the tireless crimson and blue
of Christ in Glory ...

~

Here am I, watching
from cover, as if the story –

this 'sequence of events' –
might somehow be told without me.

I've placed myself inside the Lady Chapel,
where a landslip has hurled

flagstones up to the altar, for all the world
like a huddle of penitents.

~

The men cross our eyeline, pit-a-pat.
The other says, 'If you cut

a section through the hill, peeling back
the turf, you'd see just where –'

And certain music attends all this,
and lights, and strains of choirs.

iii The Slab

Sure enough, it was
that sharp-nosed type
from *The Anatomy Lesson
of Doctor Deyman*,
his own man, now,
and hard at work
on a DOA.
'Whatever roosts in their ribs
is what you're after,'
he said, and dibbed a probe
between the meat and bone,
disturbing some sort of bird
which flew straight
to the pavement-lights
trailing a spilled
sip of fluid and a line of gut.
'Which means what?'
he asked, supposing I could tell
scavenger from harbinger.
Whenever the two-tone howl
of the saw let up
we could hear those wings
drumming the glass.

'I still remember the glib
flob of Joris
Fonteyn's mind as it piled
into my bowl ... His last

thought glowed for a moment
on the brass.
It seemed a divided thing:
the nip of the rope on his neck-
hairs; a girl he once
loosened with his tongue.'

IV The Caves

Level one, you could hear the pump
like a two-stroke
engine, *rack-rack-rack*.

I imagined a messenger, toecaps
turning the gravel
as his bike puttered up to the wheelhouse.

'Sign this – ' The sun
cartwheeled across his visor.
' – use one of the man's many aliases.

Keep it by you; there's nothing *wrong*, it's just
memorabilia … if he ever
gets back, if he ever remembers a thing.'

~

Level two, it came to me
as a beach-party bass-line; I guessed
at fifteen couples, fifteen or twenty, each

perfectly matched, eyelashes,
eyebrows, hair … They danced
side by side, strung out along the tideline,

exiled from the casinos
and half-way houses, six-packs stashed
in pools, speakers set up

on a flange of rock in a shallow cave or lean-to,
where a few might stay
to sleep – *Was that the drift*

from their fire? Could the music sift
intact from shingle to shale? –
and wake next day to a bare

wilderness of sea and white horizons,
their elbows and heels
touched by mould; eyelashes, eyebrows, hair ...

~

Level three was like standing
under the perfect O of a ten-ton bell
as the sledge swung in and struck

the rim; the sound would fill
a cathedral or your skull.
It would put you on your back.

Just here it was all thin air.
Two hundred feet above
my head, a tremor

swilled the cliff-rotunda, shrill
as the voices of my companions:
Enough, far enough. Far enough.

~

Later, the sound was lost.
Not that I heard it stop, but I heard
the silence. Now it was hand over fist

to the bedrock: a low
cavern narrowing, step by step,
to a dark stream in the vee.

I was trying to follow its drift
with map and torch
when something like the soft

wallow and knock of punts
had me up and shining
my light against the current.

It was the dead, laid out,
lids off, grinning singletons
well on their way ... No one

I knew, or else no one
I missed; and just
the backwash, *lip-lip*, and nothing after that.

v The Vintner

My first time in Chateauneuf-
du-Pape, so hot
that everything seemed battened down,
roads hammered flat by it,
doors slammed across by it ...

He took me into a room
of twilight, where the cicadas
could still be heard (just)
then through to the five-acre, bone-
dry cellar, its glimmer of glass,
blue-green, its visitors crossing,
recrossing
through tunnels and herringbone arches,
like rowers in boats.

The chill was too deep for echoes.
I sampled the dozen grapes
from the dozen vineyards – the secret, it seems,
of how the darkness is blended,
furling my tongue like a leaf
to get the particular
earth, the particular growth,

when I saw them lodged
on the rim of an upright tun:
her last letter, last photo, last favour,
a Kleenex, smudged
with the indelible *O* from '*Okay*',

the nib of a fingernail,
hair from her hairbrush, a rub
of dust from the very nook of her eye.

vi The Curator

Everything under glass and still as stone. Where an item was
out on loan, a photograph gave its likeness: at a glance
you'd own they were little but horn and bone. 'I'm busy
just now,' he said, 'why not go on alone? You can't get
easily lost. Those arrows will bring you home.'

This is the razor that turned on its owner,
this is the finger that fired the first shot,
this is the flower that poisoned its wearer,
this is the riddle that started the rot.

But when I turned the corner, he was there; of course he was.
'Aren't we a pair?' he laughed, as if climbing the stair in step,
as if breathing that mouldy air, might make us sudden
partners in Truth-or-Dare. He thumbed the catalogue; the
sheer size of it made me stare: the weight of loss. 'Is it
something particular?' As if he didn't know. 'Is it something
awry or unfair?'

This is the poodle that bit Aristotle,
this is the tongue with the strawberry wart,
this is the rattle they found in the shtetl,
this is the cutie who wouldn't abort.

He stood at the door to see me off, and wore the cloths of frailty like the Godless poor: which fooled me not one bit. 'You've seen damn-all, you know, but if you're sure – ' He snicked the ID off my coat and tore the lapel a token inch. 'A souvenir ... ' Now I no longer wore my face and name. 'It's queer,' he shook my hand, 'this way or that, they all come back for more.'

This is the tumour that grew like a rumour,
this is the rafter and this is the rope,
this is the drama that buried the dreamer,
this is the hope beyond hope beyond hope.

VII In the Catacombs

I arrived with the things
I'd salvaged, like someone getting clear
of a fire, and clutching
what people clutch,
while he came empty handed;
perhaps a touch
of smoke-black around the eyes
himself, and a voice
that could pick locks.
'Am I the man
to show you the catacombs? I am!
I could walk those galleries
in a blindfold, every inch.
Ask me and I'll do it.'

~

They made a tidy row, loose-limbed
in sackcloth and roped together,
five climbers about to go
at a difficult pitch.
Others were stacked
like cordwood, bundles of heels
and toes you might take
for a growth of fungus, as ready
to fall to the touch ...
Over here were the famous twins, got up
in broderie-anglaise caps

and party frocks,
still holding hands; just here,
the Countess Leila Lorenzo,
wide-eyed at the glass
as if she had come awake in her *wagon-lit*
to silence, a lightless night,
herself the only person left aboard.

~

One such stood alone, tipped back
on his heels in a rough-cut niche.
His fine moustache had slipped
under the crust of his lip,
but his nightcap sat
full-square with its tassel intact.
My guide stopped short and got
a toehold on the stone.
'Look at the noseless bastard – '
(pushing his face
up to that dry decay) ' – have you nothing
to say for yourself
but *jaw-jaw-jaw*?' Then he took
a hand in his own, mine too,
and danced us down the racks
and rotting pallets,
collecting the climbers, collecting
the twins, through chambers
of caves, our footfalls
smacking up puffballs of dust,
collecting a bishop,
collecting a doctor, a judge, a dictator,
dancing us down

the paths and passageways,
collecting a general, collecting a movie-star,
and I heard his voice
over the din of bones: 'Can you tell
the music at all;
has it come to you yet?'
Not a note to be heard; only the skirl in my head.

~

Something akin to the tune
heard over again
from the busker who liked to work
the Vaudeville queue from the kerb:
a beggar's coat, his pipes like a hackle
thrown back on his shoulder, his boots
in a swill of booze and diesel and just a black
grosgrain tab
for his buttonhole ... Remembering that,
I saw a lick
of phosphorus,
that grew to the flickering EX
of EXIT. He whacked
the rocker bar
and shouldered the double-door,
then danced us out
to the street, collecting
the sleepers from doorways, the porters,
the fast-food chefs,
collecting the strip-joint barkers, the night-
shift workers,
collecting the junkies and drunks,
collecting the whores,

till I took my hand back and stepped
aside from the line
of the dance: which came
as no surprise to him. He wagged his head
and gave out a lippy grin, enough to say,
'Not quite what you hoped for? Well,
no one is gone for long
from a place like that.
And now that you know the way . . . '

VIII The Double

They were listed under *Sisters of the Night* –
fanciful, I thought, a touch
too feisty, but her voice
drew me on, as if
she might have laid hands on me before.

Her part of town was empty,
like a place
the money has left. She called me in,
past bins in the basement yard,
to a gas fire with its bowl

damping the air, and a bed
and a singing bird. We'd had
a week of frost so hard
it shifted brickwork – 'Weather to lag
your snatch. Think of the poor cows

working the kerbs . . . Did you ask
for a drink, or not?' She wore
lycra tight as bandages
under a coney fur. When that was off,
I saw she bore a jennet's crucifix

on the beam of her shoulders, soft
turf in the pit of her back.
There were husked seeds on the bed,
dropped from the birdcage. We lay down
four-square, like mechanics under a truck.

She looked at the photographs.
'I guess I could be like her
if I fixed my hair; but not like her or her.
And Mother of Christ, I could never
if I lived my own life twice

once look like *her*.' But suddenly
she did, for the empty eye, for the half-
cocked head, as she spread and readied herself
with a dollop of spit
to her fingertips: someone soon dressed

and gone, throwing her bag on deck,
or getting the final flight, or drinking beer
at some roadside place,
better than this,
where a donkey carries its cross into the shade.

ix The Pink Flamingo

Out of the piazza
and the May Day crowd, I lolloped
heel and toe
down the first two flights.

The Blessed Damozel, or else
her certain image,
signed me in. Then down
two more for the only room.

I went to the well —
I went to the wellhead —

The floor was a wheel.
The door was a curtain of snapshots.
A lick of light
came from the black bar-mirror,

from the lilac and lime neon
logo, from the hot
cabinet, stocked
with special-dish-of-the-day.

I went to the wellhead —
I went to the wellhead and drank —

The music was loud enough
to stun mice. Either side
of the bar hung a painting, one
of a side of beef,

uncooked, eating
a side of beef, uncooked,
the other, someone laughing
under torture.

I went to the well —
I went to the wellhead and drank —

This face and that. The air
was a curdle of menthol
and menses. This voice
or that. In the steam

of the cabinet, snug between
the tarts and turnovers,
something with teeth and hair
was warming through.

I went to the wellhead
and drank to the death of me.

x Coverack

The trick was to keep things normal, or so I thought,
and what better than this – the sea on one hand,
a hillside of fern and furze to the other,
the tumulus on Lowland Point as a marker?
Everything there was part of the fair-weather future
I'd picked out for myself;
I could number the gulls and masts, I'd shifted the wind,
and just as you might expect I expected a man
in a clinker-built skiff
taking a catch of fish this side of the headland,
and so he was. As I stood to watch
he fetched in a line of mackerel bright as the day.

So with all that perfectly placed and my mind on nothing,
or nothing much, the last thing I wanted to see
was this bundle of bones and old nankeen
come clipper-clop sideways out of a thicket of whin
and onto the path, pop-eyed and stony-still
as if to face me down. What passed
between us then was the start of everything –
a crack of anger from me which the hare took up
as a token to draw me through the whin,
then down a slither of sand and shale
to the sea, where I followed her shitty scut
between serpentine pillars that seemed to stand as a gateway,
then up to my knees in water, up to my chin,
until I was breathing water and the hare
stroking away in front. The sunlight broke rods

in the shallows, a glassy dazzle,
so I couldn't tell if the hare became a man
or that bugaboo lurched up from the deeper green
to head me off, a dead one for sure, with his eyes
like peeled eggs and his mossy smile.

He took me at the elbow and barged the tide,
towing me out half a mile or more, then down
to darker water — just enough light to show
a four-masted ship canted over, her bows stove-in.
'Homeward bound,' he said, 'with a cargo of nitrates from
    Chile,
when a blizzard put us onto the Manacles reef.
The captain, his wife, his children
died at once, but the ship took her time;
most of the crew spent the night
in the rigging and froze to death.' I looked down
and there they were, birds in a leafless tree.

'What's my part in this,' I wanted to say,
'why bring me here?' Water purled in my throat
and a sound rang into the sea. He lifted a hand
and sent his fingers across my face. 'You think
we've got the wrong man? It's always possible,
but try a few questions now
to settle the matter —' as he shifted his grip to my wrist
and brought us close to the surface. 'Did someone you love
ever die, or else did you wish
someone would? Did you ever come to grief
thanks to a lie? Did your hand
ever cheat your eye? Did you ever
long for the sea as you might have longed for your bed?'

I couldn't speak, which seemed to sting him as much
as any backchat. He put his palm to my chin
and shoved my face to the skim of the sea. 'The right man,
of course you are. Now look ashore
and tell me what's there.'
Salt and sunlight gave it a grainy bloom,
the colour pretty much gone from everything,
white trees, white hills, white stones in the harbour wall,
white buildings, my wife's white face, white faces
of my children staring out across the bay
as if they might catch my eye,
already whitened by sunlight and salt,
between an acre of sea and an acre of sky.

The answer – ? The answer is – ? The answer, I thought,
is to slip this dead hand and swim
for that stony spit and the serpentine rocks,
where I fished myself out and stripped off,
laying my clothes on a whinbush
to get the sun. 'So here you sit mother-naked,
the chill of the sea still on you' – the hare dug a tick
from the scraggy skin under her jaw – 'and what do you know
that you didn't know before?' I thought of the time
I'd spent all night on the streets
with Ragabones and the rest, the meths
going hand to hand, a knife in my pocket
that would never have made the difference, but sharp enough,
anyway, to flay a hare. I stretched out on the pebbles
alongside a scree of bottles and cola cans
and closed my eyes to it all. She clattered round
and hit my arm with her foot,
hard, so I felt the nails. 'You're disappointed,
is that it? A drowned man for your education

and nothing gained? What were you hoping for?'
'Something,' I said, 'as much a nugget
as a bird's idea of flight.' 'That's what it is,' she said
and laughed out loud, 'that's just
what you'll come to, dreamless and changeless,
alone in some place like this, or one in a crowd.'

xi The Black Museum

'You'll see the garotte is a noose of cord
with a single knot that sits
under the gullet. You give a twist
to bring your man up short, then give a twist

to straighten his back and fetch a wet to his eye,
the iris plain
like a roundel in the white, and give a twist
to start a crack through the larynx. Another twist

will open that hairline up to more of a fissure,
you might call it, about which time
his face gets that red-cum-black
of a summer damson, and all the breath you've trapped

is unpicking the stuff of his lungs, *tik-tik*,
and soon enough you'd see,
were you cleric or medic or some such scrutineer,
a great, fat laugh

jump up to his face, and then how his teeth
were grouted pink and how the tip of his tongue
could fall as far as — ' while all the time
the waxwork man was looking me straight in the eye,

backed-up to the strangling-post
but set on a plinth, with his executioner
handy to take up the slack — yes, looked me full in the eye
as if to say, 'I can vouch for that,

or some of it, but what I remember best
is three-steps-up-four-down
with a passageway in between that brought me out
from my lock-up to a yard claggy with moss,

then a short, steep tunnel, a bull-run,
down to this bunker. All the way he laid
a hand to the back of my neck
like a parent bringing home a wayward child ...

Which doesn't mean I was special to him, not at all,
one of, oh, a dozen or more
that week, a dozen the next,
all tested for truth, helped with the truth, though it's true

I couldn't give a shred of it back,
nor drum up a lie
except you would laugh out loud, like him, to hear it,
then bring me in disappointment to the post.'

At about that moment, someone pulled the plugs
on the hubbub of dungeony
SFX, leaving just
the stereophonic *clop* of a clepsydra

and a dusty light
that fell straight between amber and umber
to give him a liverish look, apart from the touch
of rouge on his cheek, apart

from the dark of his eye, which even now held mine
as a door slammed somewhere
back towards the street. 'Hear that? That's how it was, that's how
it always started. If it starts

again, don't watch.' Just then that other man,
who stood at the first man's back, was measuring off
a good arm's length
when he seemed to notice me, and might have moved

a step closer, a step or two, wanting to say,
'Is it cleric or medic or some such? Or else
what in Christ's name,
tell me, what in all hell could you ever want with us?'

XII The Good Companion

Laid-up with all about me
a man could want: a stack of the cross-
hatched notebooks I always use,
a Stabilo pen,
a brand-new thriller that famously stole its plot
from *The Spanish Tragedy*, vodka,

a pineapple tub
of ice to sap (a little) the bright
fever that loosened my teeth, so I half-expected
to see them drop to the quilt
like sticky Chiclets,
laid-up like that, alone

you might say, but well provided for,
I felt a sleep coming on, so thick
I might have been sleeved in darkness; and next
fell into a dream quicker
than my eyes could close: in fact
I'd already declared for Bel-imperia

and was just getting down
past the damp in the crook of her knee
to those salty, pink petals
of crêpe-de-chine,
when a voice I recognised
had me up and out of there and back to my bed –

a hot, synaptic *zip*
that almost made me believe I'd woken up
until I saw the tattoo:
a letter to every finger neatly between
the knuckle joints,
as he collared the bottle and turned

a page or two of my notebooks. 'Just here:
is this *lorel* or *Lorelei*?' – each syllable sharp
as the detonations in ice
when you pour on vodka – 'It's plain
what's fretting you, but look,
you'll know it sure enough

when someone you claim to recognise climbs up
out of your bones
and legs it for the door
without so much as a kiss-
my-arse-goodbye, on a darkening day of "rain
moving in from the west", or even a shred of song.'

XIII   The Turning Point

A bill of lading (was it?),
a docket, or else
some kind of census; but then
(turned over: yes, of *course*) a map,
with a little bolt
from the blue sketched-in
alongside the severed head
of the four winds, cheeks a-bell;
and bottom-right, about east-
south-east, a brass-
bound chest, the lid thrown back
to show the toenail-
yellow of a vellum scroll encoded
with the magic square, abraxas,
abracadabras, all manner
of jiggery-pokery and waterworn
scholia: ... *this entire*
archipelago, as with the heart,
the human heart, divided
by 'that persistent three'
of Bysshe Vanolis ...

A mountain range to the north,
so no way out if those snow-
caps were more than mere
cartographer's ballyhoo;
then sea to the west: a flight
of fish, a buxom

blond dugong, Neptune
up to his scaly hips
in a force-niner.
What else, then, but the faint
path from clifftop
to meadow, from meadow to wood,
in failing light
and under the threat of rain? —
which brought me to a gate
smothered in lichen, a tuft
of horsehair snagged on the latch.
The gate led into the wood, the wood
thinned to a garden,
the garden led round again
to the sea, where I scooped
my body-shape
from the loose, dry sand
on the leeward side of a slender spur
of granite, and slept
like a man struck down, my dreams
of nothing, naturally,
but those cryptic vigias
done on the map as tiny, cross-
hatched forms that could have been
image or imago:
the first, le bone Florence
of Rome, strung up
by her hair from the strong,
dependable bough of an English oak,
turning this way and that,
as if nosing out
my best route, which seemed to be
directly into the garden

and through the orchard
to find Horatio hoist
in the ... *arbour* (was it?
or *arboretum* ...), his wounds fashioned
in the like of a broad arrow
that brought me once more to the beach,
and the man himself
laid out as a dry diver,
and pointing me back the way I'd come.

I woke to a clear, fresh day,
a gathering wind, a sea the same
indigo as his mapping ink
— *back all the way; back the way*
you came — and a noise
ringing my ear: the scream
of something soft-skinned (was it?)
coming under the claw, or else
a mollymawk, or the wind
against that granite spur, but then
(if I turned round: yes,
of *course*) it was myself,
the sound, in that plain air, the sound
of unnegotiable despair.

XIV Bedside Manners

That micro-sleep, that fugue, that daylight dream
where, if she were Bel, I must have been a ringer
for the stiff in the garden ... and the other player
about to come on, some spook
with his dead-man's-hand tattoo and the subtle grin
of someone who's taken a peek
at the plot and knows exactly what to do.

Of course I expected to wake and find them gone; of course
in the wide, white light of day
they were either side of my bed, caught up, like me,
in the terrible scheme of things. He was tight-lipped,
carrying his news like a man with a bite of bad apple
and no more able to swallow than spit, while she
brushed back my hair with her hand and sang
a line or two of 'Tam Lin' in a voice that slipped
under my skin and wormed its way to my lights.

'Bel, belladonna, bellibone, belamour ... '
my fever-fret was doing all the talking,
nor could I tell if it happened now or then
that she sang ... *gin I had kent yestreen* ...
and tiptoed out to return in her very footsteps
with a little conical glass so thick
that it carried a twist of light between
the rim and the stem, like the candy-coloured helix
in the heart of a marble, and measured off
a finger, or maybe more, of her own urine,
amber and just at body heat.

...I wad ta'en out thy hert o' flesh ...
she sang while I raised that snifter
and sipped and washed the sip around my teeth.

'Bellona, bellatrice ...' on my tongue the authentic taste
of the Warrior Queen, of her vitals, something much like
burnt sugar, a potion against the flux, against
attacks of gripe or spleen,
against the common-or-garden hex, against all fits
of melancholy, against the even-steven risk,
going on father to son, of the sin of anomie.

— But, in this case, a sleeping-draught, or if not that,
then it must have carried the taint of her own last dream,
like the blot from blotting-paper, since it took
no time at all before they cropped up again,
she as the bald beldame, he as a priest.

'These fevers, these frets, what are they except the Fates
with a heavy dig in the ribs?' he asked. 'What else
but someone spinning a line?' —
Which was on the cards all right, as she came on
with butterfly kisses, with little bites, as he
gave me a look as you might
reach out to console or subdue, as I reached out
to get a hold on the bedstead, to make a dash
for the great outdoors, but she sang me to a standstill
...and put in a hert o' stane ... as the day darkened
with a sudden, loud rush of rain among
the fruit trees and flower beds, the garden filling,
it seemed to me, with birdsong, my first
and last chance gone to try for the window, that stretch
of chequerboard lawn up to the wicket-gate,
the lane, the street, the thoroughfare,

as she brought me back to bed, my thoughts
little, now, but feverish fits and starts,
as I heard myself speak out like a voice
from the past, as she gave me the edge
of her tongue, as he gave me the back of his hand
like a blessing, his blue tattoo, his aces and eights.

xv The Gallery

It was all in sepia except
for the man centre-left, tricked-out
in shades of clerical grey, in this case grey
being a flesh-tone too

and even his eyes were grey, looking
beyond the lens to a world where you or I
might some day be seen
mounting the three broad steps

to the 'wholly accurate' mock-up,
perhaps to hang from the cross-
piece, fingers locked, just long enough
to get their POV – coiner or cutpurse –

legs going like a runner's, because
it would be impossible, I think,
to just *hang* there, then coming down,
grinning, but a touch shamefaced,

all ready with a gag
that turns on the back-to-back proximity
of 'gibber' and 'gibbet',
before taking the rest of the tour

from rack to ruin, from pillar to post,
and getting as far as the door
but going back to look
again at the face of the man,

that dark-in-the-eye, that bloodless lip,
to wonder about his tally, to wait out
his prayers, to watch him
rig the thing, to hear him say,

'Sir, you must go to this gear,'
and the world outside
unchanged, a breeze off the river,
another turn of the tide.

XVI Good Weather on the Lizard

This was a day when you could see to the ends of the earth
(where, in another life, I'd sworn to go),
the sea beaten-out to a broad blue lamina
as something off an anvil looks,
except for a slight tinfoil
crumple out by the Manacles,
and me with my back to the white sea wall
like a drifter with nothing about him but a sub
from the last odd job, and a hand of snaps,
and a 'piece of protection' – something (I'd guess) in the shape
of the skinning-knife I carried in my cuff
day and night when I kept company
with that ragged crew, on the road, or bedded-down
(one deep night of frost) in the mouth
of a storm-drain along by a river-jetty
where ... *in diesem Saus* ...
came snaking across on the swim like water-lights,
and the pick of the bunch, his balaclava
showing only eyes and teeth, his mittens
showing only the knucklebones, turned his back –
an open invitation – and led me off
into that pre-cast vault, just room enough
to stand, at first, a thin, brown twist
of water and silt at our heels,
until the pitch grew steep, and I heard the hiss
of carbide lamps, at which point he came to the lip
of a shaft and set his foot on the uppermost rung
of an iron ladder, then sank to the waist in darkness,

pausing only to ask, 'Did you ever see
a place like this before? Did you dream it up
or find it in some fancy? Did you then go down?
Can you say what happened next?'
We came into a gallery: plates and rivets,
carbide crackling like a fuse,
the whole thing high as a house and cobbled with rust.
We weren't the first. Some Jack-the-lad with a spraycan
had tagged the girders and left his handprint,
index finger out; but, just in case
we missed the point, had also made his mark
in the shape of – *Bugs Bunny?* – no, a running rope
of hares, as if it were frame-by-frame footage
of a single hare at full stretch, that lithe leap-and-tuck
taking us step by step into the tall
grainy-grey slabs of shadow between the lamps.

Each step falling away. Each shadow closing
at our backs like a door. My best bet, I thought,
was to keep a grip of the man's coat-tail
as things got darker and narrower, and the sound
of our boot-heels on the ironwork gave back
a mash of echoes … and then the echoes ended,
like a dropped pulse-beat
that never picks up, and I was walking blind,
boxed in left and right by walls
that gave off the jissom-and-linen tang
of severed roots, and a dampness grew in the air …
Not only walking blind, but walking alone,
my hand still out for the pinch
of his hem but, suddenly, nothing there to hold,
as I came up short against the facing wall
of what seemed a cul-de-sac, as if someone

had downed tools at that very point, tipping
his hat away from his brow, and sat
with his back to that final wall, that utter
full-stop, to light up, swig at his flask, unlace his boots,
thinking, perhaps, *A man can go just so far* …

The odour of severed roots, also the odour of loam.
Darkness on all sides, and a silence
so dense it seemed you might weigh it, might even speak
of 'the atmospheric pressure of silence', until
you yourself grew so rapturously still
that you could hear beyond it to the whisper and creak
of creatures working the earth … Not you, however, but me,
now lying full length to get the better air,
and putting my mind to the problem of where he had gone,
that man, and how; and before too long
an idea arrived, a stab
in the dark that made me turn onto my face
and start with my elbows and knees
like a fugitive, like someone tunnelling out,
nose-down for a whiff of river-silt,
until, less than half-way back, there it was – the watergate
that anyone should have seen, a scatter of light
washing its brick-built arch and raised portcullis,
… *in diesem Wetter, in diesem Saus* …
the rock and slap of a skiff riding the tide.

The watergate, the skiff, that line of song,
that *life*line, taking me back
hand over hand, the ivory smile
of my furtive friend, the rest of them sending
the bottle round … it seemed I'd been away
no more than a minute. 'And how did you find it,' he asked,
'your fits-like-a-glove, your custom-built?'

(My own questions going for nothing.) 'How did you like
your very own straight-and-narrow?' The look on my face
must have been easy to read, because
he put up a hand to stop me: 'I wouldn't let anyone
out in weather like this,' and passed me the bottle.
'Stay with us, drink with us, sleep on it, come to it
later in dreams if you must uncover
the nub, if you really want the *gist* —
which might, after all, be just
the kind of hocus-pocus dreams deliver ...'

~

The fact was I'd slipped away
into a doze. Now I came back with a bump, breathless,
as if I'd just sat down and taken a fix
on the crinkle of foam out by the wreckers' rocks,
just heard the wheedle and whine
of gulls on the harbour wall, just noticed
that the snaps in my hand had faded, unless the glare
from the sea had whitened my eye, had whitened
those faces, some I'd loved, loved even now,
and one who promised to lead me a merry dance.

XVII The Makers

It was pride and nothing else made me lift my head from the spit
and sawdust of the Prospect of Oblivion,
on my cheek
a dark naevus that married

a knobby knot in the planking. How long I'd been down
and out was anybody's guess; I'd guess
an hour or more by the state of my suit,
a foul ragbag,

by the state of my hair, a patty-cake
of my own ripe keck,
unless it was the keck of Sandy Traill
or Blind Harry, my friends in drink that night,

that ae night, every night, in fact, that I found myself
making the first full dip
into the cream-and-midnight-black
of a glass of stout, with a double shot on the side,

the very combination that left me wrecked,
face down, and holding fast to the spar
of a table leg as the room went by, or else
the floor was a wheel ... The brilliant double zero

of the Prospect's neon logogram swam up
from a two-quart pool of special brew, and I looked
deep for any chance reflection
of Sandy's turnip head, his docile grin, I looked

in hope of a glimpse of Harry's silver-backed
pennyweight dark glasses, taken off, sometimes, with such
graceful delicacy that Harry seemed
to be setting aside a near-impossible burden, taken off

to give you the benefit
of a baldfaced stare from a couple of weepers white
as the little scalp from a soft-boiled egg, but when
I got to my knees, to my hands and knees, to my feet,

it was just me and the barman, whose face I'd seen
before in another place, but this time kinder and wiser
as he drew me off
one on the house 'to stiffen your backbone,'

he said, 'to loosen your joints,' which put me in mind
of Sandy going down to a Scotch handshake
followed fast by a boot-heel laid
to his kidneys, one of those luminous nights

when you say the wrong thing to the right
person, 'Or perhaps the other way round,' Sandy wondered
as I held a staunch to his face in the closet bathroom
of what he liked to call his 'atelier'

with its bright blue Pompidou pipes, with its half-glass roof,
with a full moon, that night, in a clear sky, and Sandy bearing a
     pint
of blood, at least,
crusted to his shirtfront, and Blind Harry

tapping round in a stark flash-flood
of moonlight, until the ferrule of his cane
knocked the neck of a bottle of Famous Grouse. Remembering
     that,
I remembered a day spent walking the towpath

from Hammersmith down to Kew, a bottle going between us –
this would have been the day
of Francis Bacon dying in Madrid, if not
the day after for sure – and Sandy toppling back

through a common-or-garden fig as we passed the pagoda,
the bottle upraised, his complaint: 'The dearth of great
    painters.'
That was a night when none of us went home
to our beds, a night of trial and true confession

as Harry lashed out at himself,
a long, torn, *basso profondo*, sick at heart,
counting off the betrayals, the betrayed, the white nights
returning in wastefulness, the pledges, the pacts,

the business of going cold turkey, the equally tricky
business of turning a blind eye, turning a blind
corner only to find yourself
standing where you stood but ten years older ...

This was right through the dead hour of the night.
Much later, Harry said, 'In the days when I had my sight,
all I ever feared
was what might tap my shoulder in the dark.'

Thinking back to this, one foot in the neon slop,
the other hoicked on the bar-rail,
it came to me in a rush, along with my third or fourth
pick-me-up, that what Sandy had said that day

was not 'dearth' but 'death',
a thought I chased to the mirror behind the bar
and there he was, the Old Man, larger than life, his eye
like a raptor's, raw and quick, who took

Bacon that day in Spain, who took Soutine
and Schiele and Rouault, three who knocked me flat
before I could think, before I knew a thing,
leaving me no way back

and took John Keats in a room by the Spanish Steps,
stanza della morte, where I caught
one glimpse of the flowered beams and fainted fast,
and took Pierre Bonnard

who delved with me deep in the mysteries
of domesticity, year in, year out, leaving me no way back,
and took the 'Tam Lin' poet, took
the poet of 'Jellon Grame', and took my friend

'Henri de Beaufort', self-styled,
who introduced me first to Jeanne Duval, leaving me no way
    back,
while Baudelaire brayed from his deathbed
— *merde merde merde* — and took

Kirsten Flagstad, who delivered up
Kindertotenlieder, a gift outright, the radio on
as I leant from my bedroom window to smoke that night,
that ae night of sleet

and little light and a frozen sea,
brass-bollock weather as Sandy would no doubt have it,
when even on pain of death
I couldn't have told you who in hell was Mahler

or Rükert, and took
Alberto Giacometti, who said, 'The more
I take away the bigger it gets,' thereby
explaining a lot and leaving me no way back, and took

the distant greats like dominoes, *not dearth
but death*, and took Serina Stocker,
who taught me how to flay a hare ('You get
the knife under her scut – see there? – then up

over the paunch, enough to peel and pull,
and it's off like a Babygro'), and took, within a week,
George Stocker who said to all,
'I shall turn my face to the wall, and there's an end,'

and took Giacomo Puccini, who sent me
crying from the hall, too green and feverish
to be clever, and took, one day, a mere face in the crowd,
who fell or stepped

onto the rail, and was brought back up
broken, wide-eyed, a fallen angel, and passed,
like our best ambitions,
from soiled hand to soiled hand,

and took Albert Camus
who dressed me in black and told me to grow a beard
and pronounced me an *Existentialist* through tears
of laughter, and took Sigmund Freud

who sat at my shoulder throughout one bookblind summer
foxing me utterly, and took,
one by one, like a circle closing a circle,
people I should have loved

but wouldn't, leaving me no way back, and took
Walt Whitman and Dashiell Hammett and Thomas Kyd,
who hitch-hiked with me
through France and Italy and down to Greece,

the four of us with our toes at the utter brink
of a strip of dual carriageway a mile
beyond the city limits, backed by cornfields,
and darkness coming on with a mist of drizzle,

took them as he's bound to take
whoever might catch his eye, and there's an end
that even the brightest must come to, even the best,
as with the wynd wavis the wickir, even the great

and good, 'Even your good
self and my good self,' the barman said, putting a cloth
to the mirror where now only a tarnish lay,
nickel and muffled yellow just below the glass, an end

even for Sandy and Harry, two faces
I'd hoped to see again, but he pulled me 'one for the road' and
    next
I was through the door, the last swallow
still caught in my throat, and walking the precipice

of a four-lane freeway, hearing Whitman's line again
in the beat of an engine
half a mile back, hearing Sandy say,
'There comes a moment when you lay your brush to the canvas

and everything's *ease*, everything's *gift*,
so that even the time it takes
to load your palette is unendurable boredom,' whereupon
Harry turned his head, as if to darkness.

This was just before dawn and the whisky gone.
Much later, I came to see
what Harry might have meant by that sudden
turn-and-shudder, not least as I shuddered in turn,

tenant of that stinking suit, not least
as I bowed my head to a brisk downpour, not least
as the road unravelled
behind me, leaving me no way back, not least

as I considered those days of dog
eat dog ('just blanks' in Sandy's view, 'just blanks', by which he
    meant
canvas, or *pages*), the yards of unread books,
the music stalled on 'pause'

in a room that no one uses any more, my face in the glass
of *Femme debout dans sa baignoire*, the sea rising
off the sea wall with a cold, mechanical hiss, the days dug in
when even the clear

prospect of money couldn't raise the dead-
weight of a way of life gone out of fashion,
days of certain folly, certain fools, a certain
landmark standing out of a day-long mist, the interest

you pay hand over fist, a certain way
of simply getting down the street, a sense
of things going under, a sense of things running to waste,
the knack of living always against the grain, the stinging glare,
    that day,

of the city in negative (just blanks)
as my plane tilted and dropped and I saw the sun
on a stretch of water, nickel and curd yellow, like a stain
under glass, a stain

under the fingernail, not least as I turned that night,
that ae night, and cocked my thumb at a slow-lane juggernaut
decked out with coloured lights like a carousel
and rolling up through the rain.

XVIII A Room with a View

I knew her at once: I'd've known her anywhere
from the thumbnail sketch, a fair
likeness in phone-booths, in clubs, in pubs

just at eye-level (for the average man)
on the pepper-and-salt roughcast
above the urinal

so you caught her name and number
in the very moment you laid a hand to your dick
and then you'd be stuck, your focus fixed

on Mlle Stiletto, or else
Dominique, Domino, Dominatrix.
Whoever you wanted most. Whoever racked you best.

Never before or since … That was her boast
as she set her lips four-square
against your lips to give you a taste

of paradise lost,
the very taste you'd agreed to forswear.
Not me, however; I was there

to put her to the test, and that I did,
working her through each *nom d'amour*,
Delilah, Delores, Deluxe,

until we must have passed a jigger of spit
between us, a jigger
if not a bumper, which left me laid out

and counting stars
in the glimpse of sky you get
from her basement window unless she pulls

that roller-blind with its blinding
trompe l'oeil window open
to a morning you might have opened your window to

twenty or thirty years ago, the sun
red-raw like something skinned,
the sea sharp blue, breakwaters, a beach, the bright

white scarp of a cliff, a cave shelving off
steep as a mineshaft,
and someone about to make the dark descent.

'. . . or I could just as well be myself . . .'
as she came back in with Absolut and ice
on a lordly dish, making space

amid the pilferage and pelf ('All in a day's
work') and when she enfolded me, herself
was who she became: her sudden blondeness,

the strawberry blaze
on the boss of her shoulder, the light line of down
that ran to the point of her jaw, the hang

of her head, when she enfolded me, the fold of her knee,
the crêpy quoit of her arsehole,
the crêpe of her footsole.

XIX The Impostor

I was going lightfooted, my strong ambition
to be just a face in the crowd since the recent kerfuffle

with a ticket-inspector who saw me getting through
to the platform by the only gate

marked EXIT, my mind still fixed
on that oddness a moment before when I found myself

buying my one-way ticket
with a credit card made out in my father's name –

a man who paid spot-cash
all his life, but there it was with its flash

silver hologram
of a bird in the hand, and nothing for me to do

but forge the *Albert Edward* and step aboard,
dawdling hardly at all

in the buffet-car with its tiny tots
of whatever takes your fancy over ice, its hot

cabinet, its steward in starch and braid (who must
have been the cousin or brother

of that ticket-collector who gave me all the bother)
before finding the *wagon-lit*

of the Countess Leila Lorenzo, her window blinds
drawn on darkness, who drew me down

for sawdust kisses right and left to the face;
and thus we sat, and thus

we travelled, an hour or so, until our pace
and rhythm changed to the giveaway clatter and lurch

of the points as someone somewhere threw a switch
that took us off on a spur

to Christ knows where, I thought; and, looking out,
saw the walls of a tunnel, sloping down,

and saw the platform, and saw the flagman swing
his lantern; and after that

we walked, still on a downward slope, the Countess
breathing fast and leaning

fiercely against my arm, a little
rip-rip-rip as the ferrule of her cane

went in among the clinker, a little *clak-
clok-clak* as her hip

fell in and out of joint, and I matched her brittle shuffle
the only way I could, with a military slow-step,

one foot raised for a beat
of three, then down, then up with the other,

and thus we walked as the tunnel opened up
into arches and architraves and herringbone pillars

where tables were set with crystal
and silver, the linen glowing in the gloom

like the bindings of Christ, the whole crew there
to greet me, their mildew and motley,

as a flunkey stepped up with canapés and a flute
of Veuve Clicquot, who might

have been the twin of the man in the buffet-car
or that other sicko

who roughed me up at the gate,
but before I could call him back it was time to sit

and eat, after which it was time
to get up and dance: *So your hand if you would*,

and I led the Countess
lightfooted onto the floor where she gave me first

the benefit of her mossy smile, and next
an almost motionless waltz, *clak-clok*,

and thus we danced, except
soon enough he was on his way back, the quick-

change artist, to ask:
'Is it you? With that touch of gel to your hair

and the jawline starting to blur,
I couldn't properly tell. For a start,

is it your name we have here' – he held
the counterfoil, the counterfeit – 'or that

of *Albert Edward*, a man
you much resemble, or so it seems to me?' At which

I swung out a blow
that would have made a horse pull up and drop

but he sidestepped that
and fetched me a bony backhander,

that set me on my rump amid a slop
of champagne and diesel, which mix itself was a sort

of Proustian kick-start, so the day came back
as a series of dumb vignettes in crosshatched black

and white: the gate,
the train, the tunnel, the flagman, my father's face

in the hologram, a grim
none-of-your-bastard-poetry look that might have been

his death mask for all I know, for all I saw of him
at the last, the feast,

the dancers in a ring, the Countess and me
making our slow way back, her stick

tapping the track, my step,
remember, one to three of hers, and my ears well-pricked

for a sound of singing along the line, though I heard only
the *plak-*
plak-plok of seepage and spillage,

until we reached the spur and I could see
light at the end of the tunnel

which meant about as much
as it ever had; and then: *Your hand, if you would —*

reaching out with her own
for a handshake, a handclasp, that seemed less a fond

farewell than a bond as she addressed herself
again to the dark, a rank

tunnel-dew settling white
on the latch-lace of her veil like frost

on a web, and a whiff
of her bowel on her breath when she turned

to give me good day and point me off with her cane:
'Albert ... you know the way ...'

xx The Old Curiosity Shop

'You won't find much,' he said, 'on what you might term *le bel étage*: andirons and such, nick-nacks for niches that brand of persiflage...' Also a bell-shaped cage (Swiss, or else Dutch) with a tin-and-feathers-touch-and-go *carduelis cannabina*, beige-backed, blush-pink about the breast; also this bottled ketch; also this hutch, a pill or two of dung firmly attached to the obit. page of the old *Sunday Despatch*.

So it's down to the Bargain Basement and fifty quid the pair for a set of novelty bookends: the hanged man and the hare.

Also a clock. Also a trunk with a hasp-and-butterfly lock for safe secrets. 'You look,' he said, 'like nothing so much as a drunk coming up for air and taking stock.' He shook my arm. 'This is just junk. Even that fake baroque timepiece –' Then I was sunk; I knew the rest: '– has lost its strike,' I agreed, moving the hand along, glad hand, dab hand, to the final stroke. Clunk-*clunk*. Hear that? Tock-ti-tock-ti-*tock*.

So it's down to the Bargain Basement for something rich and rare,
Albert Pierrepoint's necktie and Gary Gilmore's chair.

Also an Ink-Flo pen set, its marbled shank, its phial of Quink.
Also a dolphin lamp. Row upon row, all the old stuff. He
laughed: 'I simply can't think –' Also a top, a cap, a crop, a
sack of snaps, a double blank from Waddington's *Truth or
Dare* ' – why you should hanker,' he dropped a wink, 'after
this or else that –' Also a folio, lightly foxed, of Doré's
engravings for *Paradiso*. (Also that clock.) ' – since what
you might term the nonpareil, the rara avis, is always kept
below. What you might term the absolute rinky-dink.'

> So it's down to the Bargain Basement, and what should we
>   find there
> but ratchet and cog and a silly smile, topped off with a
>   hank of hair?

XXI Lucky Dip

Hairs from her hairbrush, dust from the nook of her eye:
the figure-flinger's stock-in-trade
you might call it. A page from my manuscript.
Her likeness. Her signature.
I reached down into the tun to get the rest.

'But that's not cream in your coffee –'
This was my long tall friend with the jaundiced view.
' – no, that's not cash in the bank.
You with your arm right to the armpit
in the bran-tub of likely images
and the best you come up with is that – and that, and that.'

All the old stuff I thought I'd thrown away …
'What you need at this stage of the game
is not these trifles, these taps
on the shoulder, so much
as those certainties that lift the human heart.'

His voice carried echoes in among the racks
and brought a recollection of the place
before the rot set in,
root and crop, before they drank the last drop,
and at once I got the sudden, chalky smell
of rain on summer streets and saw,
as if for the first time, that handprint on the wall
where someone had leaned to scrutinise the ochre
and cobalt cameo
of one creature about to fall on another's neck.

I stood flatfooted, then, like a dowser
who, against all reason, feels
in his bootsoles the tug of something swift and deep.
'What you need is not so much
a place to come to as a place to start.'
Those certainties that waste the human heart.

XXII The Locket

When I came up for air, the party
was going a gallop under a starry sky,
beach flares and oil-drum fires, a sound-system with speakers

the size of wardrobes, jacked-up
to a generator
and spreading a bass-line that seemed to throw a shudder

into the overstretched undersides
of the waves at the very moment (think
of the uttermost top of a yawn) when they folded and pitched

onto the tidewrack – bobbing bottles, jellyfish condoms,
the sort of stuff that arrives on the evening tide
after an all-day bash aboard some yacht

where the girls lie bare-arsed
on the foredeck, bare-arsed on the wheelhouse roof, while the
    men
make ship-to-shore calls and, even as they speak,

you can watch the broad, bright, sky-high tracks
of flight-capital on the move.
This party wasn't like that. This party was more like the party

before the end of the world, from the way the dancers
danced, the way the drinkers drank, the way certain stars
    picked out
their place in the heavens, but first of all from the way

a hare stood plainer than day in the seas of the moon
like a die-stamp on a silver brooch
or locket, which perilous vision was quite enough

to lead me first to a drink, then into the dance
where I found myself seeing
eye to eye with a certain girl who wore just such a locket

over the ragged splash
of a strawberry-mark that went by the point of her jaw
to her throat and down the dip

of her collarbone, like a blush or the start of spoilage in fruit
—*All this in the light of that hunter's moon. All this in the light
of what had gone before* —

whose face (I felt) I might have recognised
had we stayed by the shoreline fires, but she danced me up
the shingle and down

to the darkest part of the cave
where I'd surfaced only an hour or so before,
and shrugged off her pelt, as I could have told you she would,

and bedded down on the naked rock, myself
at her side all night,
sleepless, or so it seemed to me, except that I woke

to sunlight shoved up
like a door against the cave, and nothing, now, of the dancers,
the music, the fires, that girl, not a sign, not a scent,

until I got to my feet and took stock, and found,
right there on my soft
underbelly, the perfect reverse of that strawberry dab —

the Rorschach blot
that everyone reads as a moth, or some creature
expertly flayed, or two figures, hooded, arms raised to wave
   you off.

XXIII An Experiment

He must have been standing just there,
just *there*, like *that*,
two hundred years or more
unless I'd slipped
in through the door a couple of minutes
after the others had left;

in any case, he was alone
staring at something
everyone else had missed, his eye
so hot for the quest, you'd think it
the eye of a loon,
the rimless eye of a prophet,

taking a view of things that went all the way
to the other side of the room,
and that glimpse he'd recently had
of whatever it might have been:
America, Andromeda,
the back of his own head.

I could see the bird was stone dead.
'And what's this,' he fanned the crisp
white crest with a fingertip,
'but the residue of stars, the final jot
from each of a million stars, an old star-
system emptied of its light? —

isn't that what we come down to,
in the end?' He gave a nod
at the specimen jar, the dark gizzard
in its formalin soup:
'But there's hazard in knowledge. This odd
fellow bled all ends up.'

Unlike the white bird. It lay
on his hand, unblemished
except, perhaps, for the awkward way
its beak clapped its tongue, and the one
broken feather, and the reddish
bloom in that far-seeing eye.

XXIV Up for Air

Imagine two men, one of whom, after all,
must have been myself. Imagine some small

bird, perhaps a wren,
bumping the infinite structure of the rose

window again and again, in something
like rapture, while the men

rope up towards the borehole, nose
to nose, seeming to cling

to the mere idea of themselves. Got the picture?
Well, imagine part of the tackle

failing, as if some fickle hand had chosen
to loose its grip and wag

a finger at the whole mad enterprise.
Imagine the look in his eyes,

that other man, imagine his frozen
cry, the sound of less than nothing at all,

as he pitches up against
the flagstones in the Lady Chapel.

~

'If you cut away
a section of my sleeve and peel it back,

you'll see just where – '
Which next I did, laying bare

the bits and pieces of a greenstick
fracture. He chuckled. 'No clean break:

you might have guessed as much, you might
have imagined some similar touch of fate,

the juggernaut jack-knifing at the cross-
roads, the surgeon who arrives a minute late,

the rock-hard block of piss
released from Alpha Foxtrot at the rate

of thirty-two feet per second squared
and some poor pilgrim

lifting his eyes to heaven in the slim
hope of a just reward ...

Leave me here – ' (backed up to a fresco, thanks
to my straddle-and-drag technique)

' – I'll catch you later;
your thoughts and mine are like links

in a chain, don't you think? As intimate
as the count-down in hide-and-seek – '

(A fresco, I should have said,
that airborne acids would soon obliterate:

even now it had faded
to not much more than a set of peek-

a-boo ribs and a skinny grin, and then
a cleric's wig, a medic's bag, and what might have been

the mitre and gaiter
of a bishop about to join the dance)

' – close as a hand in a glove.
Shove off. I'm happy enough. Take the water-

bottle, take the hardtack and jerky
or whatever it was you brought.

There's no real chance
of getting lost: the map's a load of malarky,

but no one could miss
the manhole of white light cut

in the cupola, or miss the sound
of sirens and engines and bells from the upper ground.'

xxv The Happy Accident

It was one of those moments when
someone's on your mind and the right
face at the right time
pops up out of the crowd, so you follow,
step for step, as he jaywalks
between the lines
of cars backed up as far as the city limits.
A day like any other – you swallow
your peck of CO_2 and cadmium;
every few minutes
a siren starts up, or a shop alarm;
a cop-car slaloms
up to a black-spot junction
and fishtails across the flow.

Your friend (unless it's his double) barely
turns his head to this racket.
He comes to a gate of bars in a redbrick wall
near the piazza, stops to unlock it,
and lets himself in to a formal
garden, with statues of hound and hare
flanking a central path
that leads like a pointing finger to a certain
door, and beyond the door, a hall,
and across the hall, a door
which (as you've probably guessed)
is the only sure way in to the sanctum
sanctorum; and that's where I found him,

still nosing the marginalia
to the minor and major arcana,
the pencilled obiter dicta ('... *a worme
cam out of his hedde* ... '), the usual picture
of a man with his pole
and bundle, a poodle or papillon
up on its hindlegs, eager to go, the untrodden
path he must take,
half-hidden by trees half-hidden
by a pall of mist from the cataract.

'Yes? And what *exactly* did you expect?'
Next thing, he tweaked
my notebook from my pocket, and flicked
the pages. 'Is this *dearth*
or *death*? Is this *lorel* or *Lorelei*?'
He licked his teeth.
'What did you think to gain
from the sights you've seen, the miles you've clocked?'
'Something,' I said, 'as much
a nugget – ' 'Oh, *that* ... ' He angled the folio
towards me. 'Look, but don't touch.'

~

The usual picture. A man, his dog, the torrent.
A place where the road forks.
You almost get the scent
of pine. He turned the page –
there was the sawbones, busy with a stiff
who'd just come under the knife;
there was the dusty grid
of pavement lights; there was the very bird,
beating against the day.

It took that familiar, dark-brown cough
to bring me back to myself.
He closed the book and smiled and spread
his hands, as if to say, 'I could
show you more; but now that you know the way ... '